God's Poiema

God's Poiema

His Workmanship
Ephesians 2:10

Roberta L. Young

WestBow
PRESS
A DIVISION OF THOMAS NELSON

WestBow Press books may be ordered through booksellers or by contacting:

WestBow Press
A Division of Thomas Nelson
1663 Liberty Drive
Bloomington, IN 47403
www.westbowpress.com
1-(866) 928-1240

Because of the dynamic nature of the Internet, any web addresses or links contained in this book may have changed since publication and may no longer be valid. The views expressed in this work are solely those of the author and do not necessarily reflect the views of the publisher, and the publisher hereby disclaims any responsibility for them.

Any people depicted in stock imagery provided by Thinkstock are models, and such images are being used for illustrative purposes only.

Certain stock imagery © Thinkstock.

ISBN: 978-1-4497-2670-6 (sc)
ISBN: 978-1-4497-2671-3 (hc)
ISBN: 978-1-4497-2683-6 (e)

Library of Congress Control Number: 2011916445

Printed in the United States of America

WestBow Press rev. date: 9/15/2011

*I*n memory of my mother, Mary Wilma Westlake, who, at the age of 75, gave her heart to Jesus, reminding me of God's prevailing grace and undying love; and Rev. D. Scott George, a constant champion of my poetry who always encouraged me to "keep writing those poems."

To my husband, John, whom God has given to be my steady rock, never giving up on me, especially through 14 years of depression. I love you; and to my children: Amber, Bill, and Jennifer, whose prayers God heard and restored me.

Contents

$\mathcal{F}oreword$

Life is a series of ups and downs with alternating periods of laughter and tears. For all, life may be amusing or it may be distressing; life may be awesome or it may be ordinary; life may be victorious or it may be overwhelming. My friend Robbie and I have shared many of these life's experiences for almost 40 years.

Although these poems reflect her journey, it's a journey with which you and I can identify. As you peruse the verses in this volume, you will reminisce about the events in your own life. Most of all, you will sense the ministry of the Father, His Son, and His Spirit in the life of the author. If you share this experience, thank the Lord with Robbie. If you cannot relate to His persistent presence, ask Jesus to be your Savior and Lord and live your life in rhythm and rhyme with Him.

Dr. June Leasure, PhD, NCSP

My first reaction to poetry is, "Poetry, that's just not for me." But then I consider my love of the Psalms in the Bible and think, "Who am I kidding? I love poetry!"

$\mathcal{I}$ first met Robbie in 2006 as part of a prayer team to Uruguay I was leading. I watched as she interacted with people, praying with tears over a country whose rate of suicide ranks extremely high, and a lack of God's good news the same. God had caught her heart for the people of Uruguay and soon became its Country Prayer Champion for the Men For Missions Prayer Initiative (MFMI). She believes God's desire—that no one be lost, but all come to the saving knowledge of Jesus Christ. So she prays down the glory of God upon Uruguay and trusts the Savior's love to reach to the uttermost.

Her poems capture that Jesus; that Jesus that loves and saves, heals and restores. This book is not to be read in a hurry. Read each poem slowly; let it resonate in your heart; let it soak your soul; let it draw you ever closer to Jesus. When you finish your journey through this book, you will better understand the Jesus that Robbie loves and wants the world to know.

Richard McLeish, Director, World
Intercessors, One Mission Society

Preface

In 1971, while holding my first born on my lap, I was overwhelmed by the love I felt for her. I wanted her to know that God, who blessed me with her, loved her even more, so I began to tell her (what 8 month-old understands 75 words thrown at her in less than a minute!), realizing each thought rhymed. Suddenly I was singing the words to her. This poem/song was to be sung quite often over the years as a mother of three—even into their teen years. The thoughts kept coming, the words becoming—poetry!

Sorrow—joy; losses—new beginnings; anxiety—peace; discouragement—hope; burdens—victories; all part of living. I have experienced all the above and will continue to do so until that which is known only in part shall be made complete by the appearance of Him who lived His life dying to save mine.

This soft-spoken, easy to read book of poetry has been inspired from a heart touched and changed by an encounter with the Living God. It is written to bring inspiration, comfort, hope, and joy to all who read.

Roberta L. Young, author

Acknowledgements

Thank you, Dr. June Leasure, PhD, NCSP, for surveying my work, assuring me it was book material. Great appreciation to Robin Zgurski, B.S. Technical Management, specializing in Business Information Systems, for designing my book cover. All graphic illustrations are by Cherie Metcalf, B.A. English, M.S. Education, who also is my editor. Without your expertise, lots of editing hours and confidence in perfecting the final draft, my poems would still be on bits of notepaper, envelopes, and napkins in a zipped-locked baggie! A true life-long friend, to you is given my deepest, sincere gratitude.

For

HIM

whose love is so sure,
so steady,

so—forever!

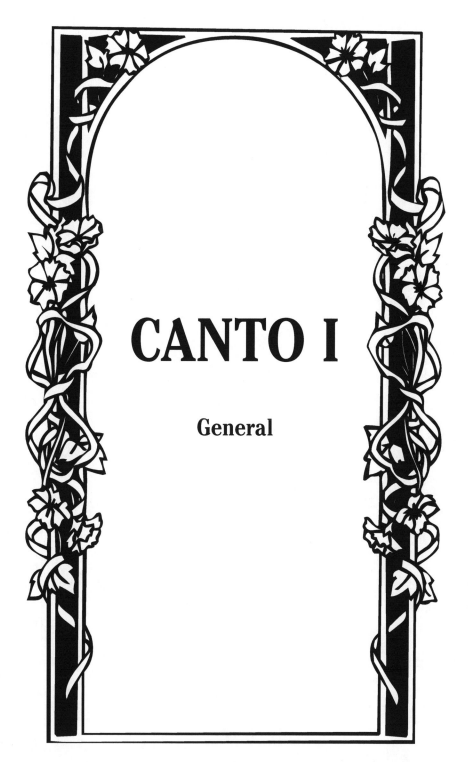

CANTO I

General

Worthy

On parchment plain with ink in hand
God pens His grace to fallen man.
Expresséd love that fills one's breast;
On Calvary's tree God gave His best.
The deed was done then He arose.
No sweeter script could man compose.
rly 2000

Resting

Naught of name that it should last;
Merely thoughts from heart been cast.
A soul once drowned in darkest sin
Forgiveness found—peace within.

Present thoughts do now express;
In Christ alone is found true rest.
rly 2002

Of Him

Light of the world
Among us right here.
Proclaiming our joy,
We shout loud and clear.
Jesus has freed us
From shame and despair.
This song of deliv'rance
We've come to share.

Now . . .
We've been forgiven from our sin—
That's why our praises are of Him.
Give God the glory as we sing.
He will deliver—He's our King!

Voices called out
And choices were made,
Forgetting the price
That soon must be paid.
God heard the cry
Of a broken-down soul;
Put back the pieces—
His love made us whole.

And . . .
We've been forgiven from our sin—
That's why our praises are of Him.
Give God the glory as we sing.
He will deliver—He's our King!

Still the world calls us
To just play its game,
But on your life
It will leave a red stain.
Jesus still loves you
And knows what is best.
Lay down your burden—
Now come and find rest.

And . . .
You'll be forgiven from your sin—
Sing a new song that's just of Him.
Give God the glory as you sing.
He has delivered—He's your King!

Now . . .
We've been forgiven from our sin—
That's why our praises are of Him.
Give God the glory as we sing.
He will deliver—He's our King!

rly 2004

Fragmented

Broken

to be made

whole.

Given to Him

my soul.

When on earth

'twas no other,

God came near,

loving Father.

Doing only what

He

could do:

Forgive of sin,

wash brand new.

Complete.

rly 2009

Melodious Rest

Bruits on a wire
Heard o'er the mire;
A sonnet so lovely to hear.
Their ode—'tis so sweet—
Not soon be complete.
The Composer so visibly clear.

Peace 'twixt the breast
Serves tranquil rest;
A sonnet so lovely to hear.
Whose faith—'tis so true—
E'er born to renew.
The Composer so visibly near.

rly 2010

My Calling

I love You, Jesus—yes I do.
Be Your witness my whole life through.

Days will pass; no time to wait.
Reach the lost before too late.
Stand the gap—willing to pray
For lost souls to choose the Way.
Prophet's vision clearly see—
Increase fold from bended knee.

I love You, Jesus—yes I do.
Be Your witness my whole life through.
rly 2000

Jesus

Little babe—ever God.
Holy child—always King.
Tender Shepherd—kind and good.
Wondrous Savior—angels sing.

Sacred martyr—blood sufficed.
Potent warrior—victory.
Son of God—sacrificed.
Lord of all—majesty.
rly 2001

Awe

Whither be Thy borderlands
Shouldst cease all hearts aspire?
Nay, Thy love is deep and wide—
Achieving all desire!
Lost in Thee to be found—
Toward certain wonder—bound.
What tongue rightly speaketh
Kind depth of All-Divine?
Yea, bequeathed Himself to wist
The great I AM is mine!

rly 2008

Surrounded

God walked to Calvary
    for you to know forgiveness.
God walked from the grave
    to give you eternal life.

Today God wants to—

Walk beneath you
    and lift you up,
Walk above you
    and keep you humble,
Walk before you
    and show you the way,
Walk behind you
    and keep you steadfast,
Walk beside you
    and be your friend.

rly 2009

Regeneration

Unseen growth and change.
Rain.
Faith.
Cold hard terrain complies
to Heaven's command to drink,
which will birth beautiful explosions of color on display for all to be
awe-struck at such creation,
that one can do nothing but
give Him glory and praise,
lifting hands and face heavenward,
only to see the reflection of His face
through the brightness of His glory.
How can one not believe?

Entering through the door of hope,
bow before the God
of Heaven and Earth.
The chamber of holiness
would consume immediately
if it were not for His only Son,
Jesus Christ.
One should remain still with awe,
save His request to come boldly.
He hears the soul speak without sound.
He transcends the consideration of
peace, joy, and love
because He is.
How can I not believe?

Unseen growth and change.
Rain.
Faith.
A parched barren soul complies
to Heaven's command to drink,
which will birth beautiful explosions of color
on display for all to be
awe-struck at such grace,
that one can do nothing but
give Him glory and praise,
lifting hands and face heavenward,
only to see the reflection of His face
through the brightness of His glory.
I do believe.
rly 2009

Image

Acts of beauty you can see;
Rainbow colors for you and me.
Stars and moon and world's beyond—
All in place where they belong.
Radiant view—sky to sod;
Clearly seen—the face of God.

rly 2004

The Father's Will

A crimson fountain makes you white.
Pure, forgiven—stand in His sight.

Not of self from sin could rid.
On a cross the Savior bid.
Broken body makes all whole.
Given life to save the soul.

Moments long He hung thus still.
Did finish the Father's perfect will.
Vict'ry came—death quite defeated.
God's right hand—the Son now seated.

His Spirit remains—giving power.
Kept each moment, every hour.
In Christ alone now overcome.
A crown awaits when race is won.

rly 2009

Sunday Sermon

Pray for the one who sits next to you;
Front, behind—pray for them too.
There may be some struggles—
Heartaches, a few.
God knows the hearts
That sit in each pew.

Pray for the Pastor,
The truth he declare:
The Cross, it's vict'ry—
The Word he must share.
God's Holy Spirit—
Let it fall and not spare.
Anoint now your servant,
This place everywhere.
rly 2006

Forget Not

Loose the tongue to boast this wonder:
He chose to come—why yet ponder?

Ready the fount did cover sin.
Justified fully—entered in.

Ah, 'tis sweet such death to recall—
Upon the altar was given all.
rly 2004

Glorious

The sun's risen—O glorious day.
Lights our path along the way.
The sun has set—O glorious view
With purple, orange, and amber hue.
The stars have lit—O glorious glow.
All such names their God does know.
The moon has shown—O glorious beam;
So near an orb that men may dream.

The Son's risen—O glorious day!
Lights our path along the way.
The Morning Star—O glorious sight!
Ever shines, dispels our night.
The Cross appears—O glorious thought!
Eternal hope our Savior brought.
Salvation's plan—O glorious feat!
Forgiven sin makes love complete.
rly 2011

Ready

East to West every eye will see.
The signs are here—
For you, for me.

Father will speak, appointing time.
Son declares—
"I've come for what's mine!"

His Bride abruptly swept away.
Be e'er watchful—
Could be today.

O wretched soul, 'tis not too late.
Repent your evil—
Do not wait.

God's Belov'd has covered sin.
The banquet set—
Just enter in.

One day soon besee in plain view.
One day soon—
Will He come for you?

rly 2009

The Voice Of Grace

O, hear the ring of God's own voice
Asking softly to make a choice.
Repel clamor of sirened sin—
Notes of ardor now hear from Him.

O, hear the ting of God's own word
Sounding rightness—
A two-edged sword.
Severs lining within the soul—
Psalms of healing
Shall then make whole.

O, hear the plea of God's own love
Chording gently from whence above.
Abhor bedlam of pitches dark—
Hear the melody of His heart.

rly 2002

Now

Confess all sin to Jesus—
Lest vanquished here today.
In Seas of Forgetfulness
He'll wash them all away.

Tarry not Decision's door
And bear His judgment rod.
Walk right through to loving arms
Of all-forgiving God.

Live for Jesus now dear one—
Don't wait for the morrow.
So soon comes the final day—
You will know much sorrow.

Watch close all prophetic signs
As on the Lord you wait.
Read His Word—prepare your soul—
Lest it be too late.

rly

Faithful

On a hill our soul was kept.
Somber sky, though God ne'er slept.
Blood was spilled—then He died.
Mercy heard man's soulful cry.

Turned not He from Father's will.
Price was paid as earth stood still.
Death was conquered—love had won.
Vict'ry given to the Son.

We rejoice He gulfed the span—
Severed veil 'tween God and man.

Promised true, He's coming back.
Some don't see—count Him slack.
What God says He will do.
Heaven waits both me and you.

Riv of Life, all streets of gold;
Things not seen—sights untold.
Redemption's song we will sing.
Humbly bow before our King.

rly 2006

The Rainbow's End

For what you are looking
Is beyond the sky
And cannot be seen with mortal eye.

You will not find
In fortune or fame
What riches are found in Jesus' name.

If seeking to gain
Hope, joy, and peace,
From worldly pleasure right now release

Jesus, the Christ,
Your freedom paid full.
To Him humbly give your heart to rule.

For what you are looking
Is beyond the sky
And cannot be seen with mortal eye.
rly 2010

The Portal Of Truth

Entrance of Your Word gives light.
Feeble minds now make well—
Freeing from the Serpent's hell.
Bring release from the night.

Futile roots, so cold and dry.
From their sin, thirsty live—
Living water we can give.
Hasten or they surely die.

Mercy drops are seen, O Lord.
Latter rains we now need—
Errant souls away we plead.
Consecrate Your spoken Word.

rly 2011

Grace

Unsuited immortal
Beseeches grace,
Ignoble to look upon its face.

Full pardon does speak
With endearing tongue.
Death sings of new life—a song unsung.

Sacrifice completed
Hallowed day;
Redemptive blood spilt—the only way.

O, rejoice blissful heart
Now arisen.
Go—own the Cross—wholly forgiven.

rly 2000

Rappin' For Life

Yo, God—
You're the man I gotta see.
Jump into my misery.
Sky-dweller, I need Your Son.
The Death Chaser—He's the one.
I need to see You.
I want to see.

Yo, God—
So much ruckus in the 'hood.
I can't hear You like I could.
Sky-dweller, I need Your Son.
The Death Chaser—He's the one.
I need to hear You.
I want to hear.

rly 2008

Choices

Then . . .

Ah, had I been there—
Would I have run away,
Or would I have been so bold
To make the choice to stay?

Amidst the angry crowd—
Would I have cursed His name,
Or would I have vowed my love,
Brave and unashamed?

Before the warming fire—
Would I have told a lie,
Or would I have chanced the truth,
Knowing I would surely die?
Today . . .

Ah, among the scoffers—
Will I take my stand for Christ,
Or will I quickly sneak away
And deny His sacrifice?

Amidst the darkness—
Will I draw all men to Light,
Or will I leave their souls
To question what is right?

Before the Lord—
Will I choose to live for Him
Who paid redemption's cost,
Or will I bed a devil's hell

And be forever lost . . .

rly 2001

Suddenly

Upon the Morning Star we'll gaze.
Before Eternal we shall kneel.
And suddenly . . .

What we were has no appeal.
No more questions to be asked.
Trials have now elapsed.
Forevermore—here at last.
At His feet all crowns be cast.

No more a misted glass we see.
Then we will know as God has known.
And suddenly . . .

Heaven's now become our home.
Walls of jasper to behold,
Pearled entrance soon unfold
Toward a city pure like gold—
In the written Word was told.

rly 2008

Come Gently, Come Softly

Cleanse, oh Father, unrightness and sin.
Cleanse, oh Father—
Dark spots within.
Cleanse me 'til I feel brand new.
Cleanse, oh Father—make like You.

Rain soft, rain gently over the soul.
Wash away pride—
Self, now control.
Steady rain on all dry ground,
Thirst be quenched—mercy abound.

Blow winds of freedom
'Til Foe takes flight—
Lifting above to live in Your light.
Winds of joy bring peace for strife.
Breathe Your Spirit—rule my life.

rly 2009

Onward To The Fray
The Armor of God

Never retreat—must be at best—
Rescue hearts in deep distress.

Buckle truth's belt, lace boots of peace—
Free all souls from bonds, release.

Fasten secure your righteous crest—
Shoulder close against the breast.

Salvation's helmet on your head—
By His Spirit you are led.

Take up faith's shield; firmly stand—
High your sword assured in hand.

Soldier, wane not; battles are won—
By the blood of God's own Son.

From those trenches, onward trod—
Praise THE GREAT I AM, OUR GOD.

rly 2008

Complete

On the Cross—a Savior see.
Died He did for you, for me.
Life He gave that we could know.
O, can it be? He loved us so!

In the grave—a Savior lay.
Yet for us He did not stay.
Heaven spoke—our Lord arose.
Grave's deep abyss forever closed.

To the sky—a Savior's flight.
Faith shall soon have its full sight.
King of Kings we'll see enthroned.
Beautiful place—our soul's come home.

rly 1989

Long Ago

Birthed low, a man child,
In a creature's stall.
Soon embraced royalty—
First died for all.

In time He spoke softly,
Humble and meek;
Deliv'ring love's message—
Pleading men seek.

But they walked foreign ways
Unto their loss—
Still He relinquished
His life on a cross.

Love engulfed darkness,
Frustrating evil—
Saved man's fate
From the bane of the devil.

Now He and His Father
Rule on their throne—
A place called Heaven
Th' redeemed call Home.

rly 2010

Deliverance
written for son, Bill

A delivered soul
From sin's dark pit—
No longer in guilt
I have to sit.

A prison of shame
Where once was bound—
My feet You raised
To fair, higher ground.

I'm forgiven much—
Though can't be known.
His blood covers all—
Now grace is home.

God's love, forgiveness,
He'll give you too.
Believe with your heart—
See that it's true.

rly 1988

Amazing Love

The Cross! The Cross!
The Cross I see!
A rugged old and lifted tree.
Astounding deed to love us so.
Amazing love—ours to know.

Once to gaze upon His face;
A tender look
Of bloodstained grace.
Astounding deed to love us so.
Amazing love—ours to know.

rly 1989

Disposed

Dark, beguiled, malicious one—
Dare supposed you could have won?
Dank, rotting, carnal tomb.
Death's pungent, biting sting.
Devoured here—overcome—
Divinely apt by God's Son.

Dark, beguiled, malicious one—
Dare supposed you could have won?

rly 2011

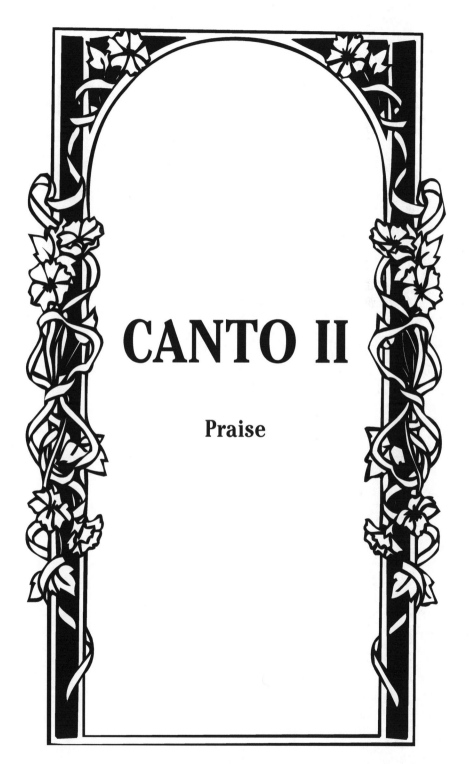

CANTO II

Praise

Give Praise

We give You glory and honor
And praises too.
Recount Your grace equally new.
Apprise Your love
The whole world through.
We give You glory and honor
And praises too.

rly 2000

Hear Ye, Hear Ye

Let the anthems ring,
The voices all sing.
Let the hands be raised,
The knee bow in praise.
Let the echoes sound,
The noise be profound.
Let the earth now hear—
Jesus is Lord!

rly

Majestic Acclaim

Hallelujah to the Lamb once slain.
Hallelujah for the King who reigns.
Praise the Father for such love.
Praise the Son who rules above.

O, hallelujah to Jehovah.
Yes, hallelujah to I AM.
He is Yahweh, Lord and Savior.
He will shield with His right hand.

rly 2010

Praise His Lovely Name

O, praise His Lovely Name.
Yes, praise His Holy Name.
Call upon God
In Jesus' Precious Name.
He can change lives
To never be the same.
O, praise His Lovely Name.
Yes, praise His Holy Name.
rly 2008

Adore Him

Habitation of splendor—
Ancient of Days.
Prostrate before Him—
Ascending hands praise.
Much adoration—
With elation we sing.
Persuade all homage
To our King.
rly 2001

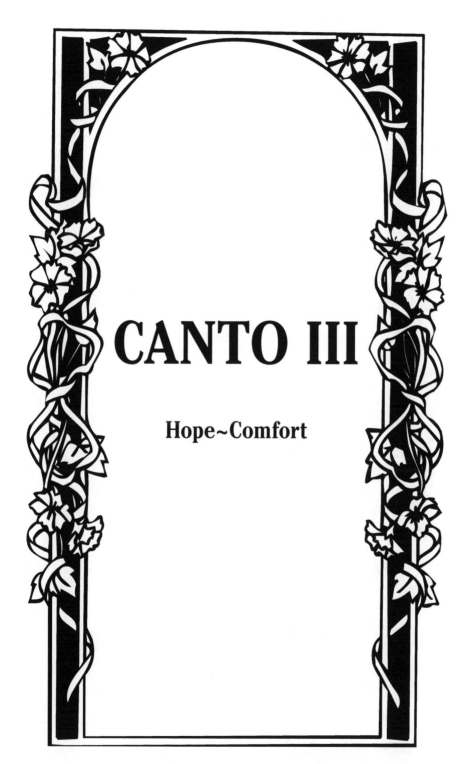

CANTO III

Hope~Comfort

Anchored

Shipwrecked, coasting—
Days into years;
Grief-torn river
Of sorrows and fears.

Drowning swiftly
In sin's murky sea,
Hope drifted by—
It anchored me.

"Up from the deep
I'll raise you above.
Reject not My heart
Nor fend My love.

Burdens I'll carry.
Sin I will bury."

No more to dwell
A gulf of despair—
Near peaceful shores
Jesus was there.

Those shattered dreams
With no hope to yield—
The Captain of Grace
Restored and healed.

rly

Together

May hope be yours while here you wait
For that glad sight at Heaven's gate;
To meet again on peaceful shore,
Hand in hand through Immortal's door.

rly 2000

The Savior's Presence

When life seems to come apart,
Let the Savior bind your heart.

When you ask the question, "Why?"
Trust in God to hear your cry.

When the sun begins to wane,
God is there to ease the pain.

When on your own you cannot stand,
He will hold you in His hand.

Day by day, each minute through,
Strength He'll give and walk with you.

rly 2008

God Supplies

Halt all fret—gain peace today.
Add joy along the way.

Cares rise great—the weight bends low.
Assist life's path to go.

Morrow's view—too far away.
Suffice all hope today.

rly 2010

Trust

God has ways we don't understand—
Carries us dear in His strong hand.

'Ere the time was thought to be—
Plans He made for you and me.

His will to do; our good, His praise—
Guides with truth to live our days.

Be not disheartened; God knows best—
Onset to finish—our surety and rest.

rly 2009

Restoration
Jeremiah 31

I have satisfied weary souls,
Renewed the sorrowed heart.
Promised hope hath been restored—
Fully whole and not in part.
My covenant of blood complete
Hath fulfilled its day.
Sure the flow of grace now floods—
Shalt wash thy sin away.

With loving kindness have I drawn;
From ages past have come.
Redemption's call heard abroad
That men repent—everyone.
Naught thy brother nor thy neighbor
Canst answer for thy sin.
Each soul shalt be beholden
To that which is within.

Now turn aside life's follies—
All thy gods thou served and chose.
Freely I wilt come to thee
And thou wilt find repose.
rly 2007

Eternal Vows

You shall miss me as I would you—
Weep awhile as I would do.
You cannot see beyond God's blue—
In God's bosom I wait for you.

I have become what I believed—
Uncorrupted—this house relieved.
The Wedding Feast He shall spread—
When our Belov'd we both shall wed.

rly 2011

An Eye For Hope

Downward staircase—free-fall.

One-way elevator—no second floor.

Gray matter—erased palette.

Familiar corner—private affair.

Shut-off valve—no response.

Retro view—senseless space.

Idle forward—choosing time.
Suggestion—

Pinhole.

rly 2011

Safe

Tantamount in the dessert place
As the oasis well.
Immutable—ahh . . . God—
An abbey to indwell.
rly 2011

God Is Nigh

The swell of the storm—it rises high;
Waves would swallow but God is nigh.

The valley is low and oh—so deep,
But God has promised ever to keep.

Safe in His love—put flight to fear;
Quiet your heart for God is near.

Deep the anguish of sorrowed despair;
Oft time seems more than we can bear.

O, be assured—'tis firm and true—
God is nigh and cares for you.
rly 2009

Hope

Depraved by sin's vulgar course,
Should one recant with much remorse?
Is mercy such that souls shall live,
Or grace, its depth, would soon forgive?

Might life exist where death lay now?
Whose love brings peace, forever vowed?
Could sacred bliss discharge all grief—
Summon freedom and bear relief?

Relieve this heart, sore from rage.
O sanction quick—pure light engage.
Complete it's chambers to become
Fierce with hope where once was none.
rly 2011

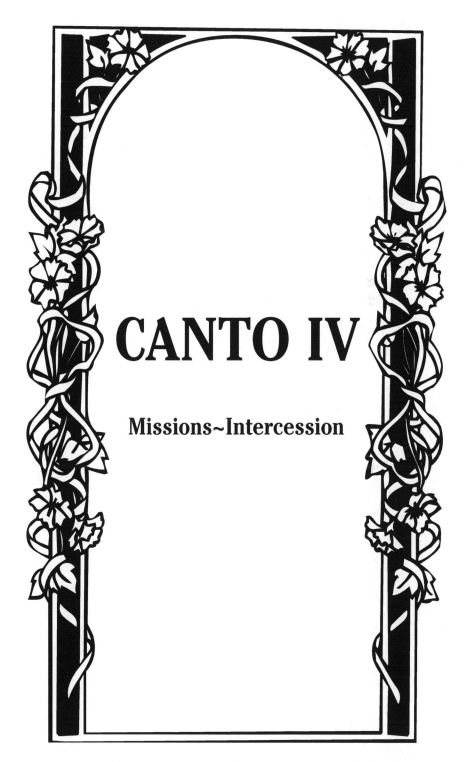

CANTO IV

Missions~Intercession

Ambassador

I shall stay for my heart grows dear
To see my Lord
Whose face draws near.
But You bid me arise
To a world of despair—
For men must know and I must share.

I shall stay for my joy is complete,
Shadowed with peace,
Fellowship sweet.
But You bid me go
In Your Precious Name—
For men perish if I fail to proclaim.

I shall stay for I see Your tears;
Man's heart has hardened
These many years.
But You bid me gather
Their souls to win—
For men need know God died for all sin.

rly 2007

Uruguay
song written for author's mission field

Open the eyes of Uruguay.
Oh, let them see and set them free.
Open the eyes of Uruguay—
Then they will know they have a Savior.

Open the eyes of Uruguay.
Come heal their hearts, from sin depart.
Open the eyes of Uruguay—
Then they will know they have a Savior.

Cause all the darkness to disappear.
Relieve the doubts
And calm all their fears.
Salvation and healing is in Jesus' Name.
Deliv'rance shall come
And God will reign!

Open the eyes of Uruguay.
Oh, let them see and set them free.
Open the eyes of Uruguay—
Then they will know they have a Savior.
rly 2006

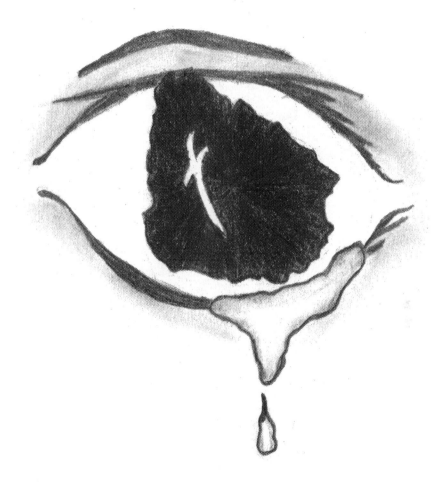

Light Of The World

How our world is dying
With sad broken peoples—
While Zion takes ease
Beneath the church steeples.

Yesteryear's lamplighter
Once lit up the night—
Need light darkened hearts:
Black, yellow, red, white.

Be the church triumphant
And share the Good News—
Do tell with such love
They cannot refuse!

rly 2001

Wait

If you do not meet with God in prayer,
How shall He lead
To those in despair?

If you do not humbly bow and pray,
How shall you know
Who's been led astray?

If you do not tarry ere His face,
How shall you tell
Of His saving grace?

If you do not stay His glow sublime,
How shall the lost
See God's love divine?

If you do not watch at least one hour,
How shall God fill
With Holy Ghost power?

God's heart is yearning
To meet you there—
In the secret place—
A place called prayer.

rly 2000

Intercession

I would my life be measured
By time spent on my knees.
A quiet place where no one knows—
A place where God lone sees.

The Spirit woes me often
And bids the soul apart;
Embrace love no other knows—
Perceive His burdened heart.

Savior sought through tears of blood,
"Now let Thy will be done."
O, to side such grief and rue—
That to the Cross men come!

Good works by faith is needed
For all to see and know.
But for pow'r to overcome—
To bended knee you go.

What is humbly sought alone
Within your secret place
Shall be openly revealed—
By mercy, love, and grace.

rly 2009

Willing

While I kneel on carpeted floor—
Urge You bless just a bit more.

Few but hear—answer the Call;
Abandon what's dear; give up all
For unknown places across the sea—
Many's the soul that needs set free.

Now when I kneel on carpeted floor—
Forgive my plea for just a bit more.
Help, instead, my town to see—
Many's the soul that needs set free.

rly 2010

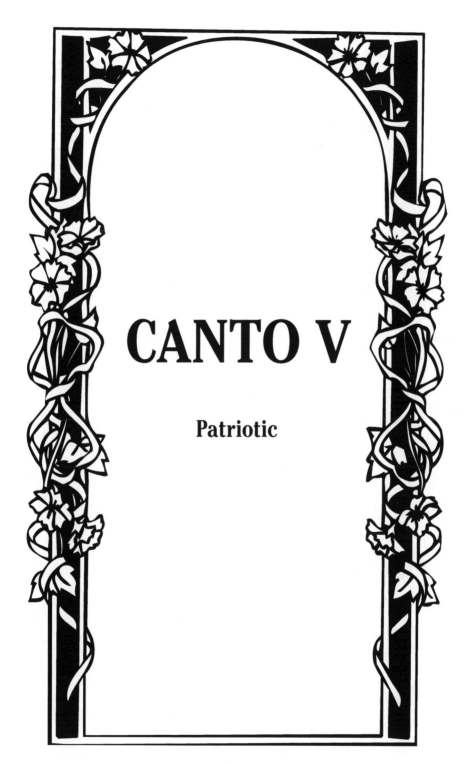

CANTO V

Patriotic

Enlisted

You're in the Army, boy!
Write often to your mother.
You're in the Army, Son!
Her love is like no other.

You're in the Army, boy!
Write to dear 'ole Dad.
You're in the Army, Son!
Best pal you ever had.

You're in the Army, boy!
You're there to keep us free.
You're in the Army, Son!
Our pride none else could be.

You're in God's Army, boy!
Been called into His ranks.
You're in God's Army, Son!
No use for guns and tanks.

You're in God's Army, boy!
Be all that you can be.
You're in God's Army, Son!
In Christ to set men free.

You're in God's Army, boy!
On earth for Heav'n above.
You're in God's Army, Son!
He'll guide you with His love.

Battles here so quick will end.
Soon made right and whole.
Then my brave and precious son,
Join the "General" of your soul!

rly 2001

America Still
9-11

Fire rages in the sky—
Shades of gray now blind the eye.

Fearful watch and question why—
There's no time to say good-bye.

Voice of truth has been disgraced—
The hand of trust now displaced.

Peaceful nation they awoke—
Collar not the foeman's yoke!

Hear dark fiend: your fate is sealed—
Freedom, honor, *never* yield!

Though we aim our soldier's gun—
Hearts declare we've ready won!

All that's lost through great sorrow—
Courage grows for the morrow.

Faces turn to Heav'n and pray—
Faith and hope will guide our way.

The One True God to be praised—
Freedom's flag still proudly raised!

rly 2001

Pilgrims Journey

Forsaking tyranny, we shall flee.
Embrace the vision across the sea.

Breathe freedom's air, so pure, so sweet.
Feel Promised Land beneath our feet.

Country were God blesses, they say—
Democracy called the U.S.A.
rly 2010

A Soldier's Peace
written for son, Bill

A warrior to foreign land I go—
Walk beside me in Kosovo.

Young man am I—
Know not what's ahead.
Will trust You, Lord, adown to bed.

Direct my steps—
O' Your mighty hand.
U.S. soldier for peace I stand.

In times feared most—
Pray see Your face.
Remind me then, Your love and grace.
rly 2000

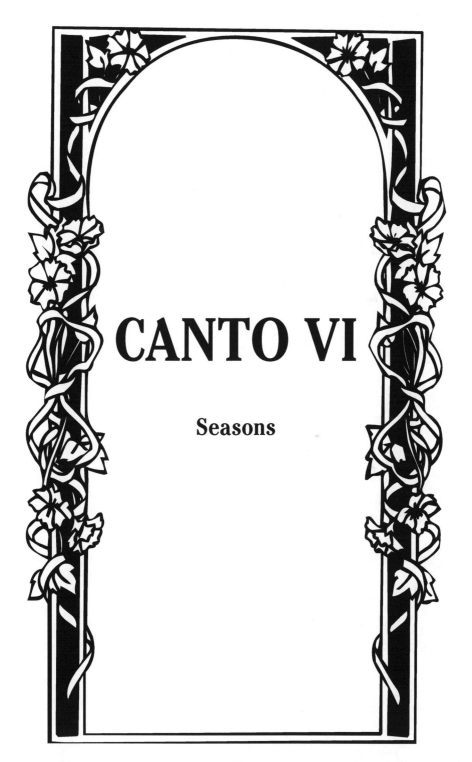

CANTO VI

Seasons

In His Time

Brought down from Heaven
By Father's own hand;
All creatures He made,
The seas, the land.

Each night, each day
He put with their season.
Displays His glory—
We are the reason.

Green leaves are changing
To red, gold, and rust.
They fall to the ground
Quickly to dust.

Windows soon frost—
Bright snow blinds the sight.
Blizzards chill bones.
Earth quilted 'neath white.

New life awakens
By first gentle rain.
Choir of feathers
Trill songs never sang.

Furrowed fields
Soon yield buried treasure.
Sun-drenched days
Are relaxed with pleasure.

Our lives are filled
With glorious swell.
The Father above
Does all things well.

rly 2002

A Winter Sonata

Mesmerized
by perfect sporadic meter.
Hypnotized
by perfect timeless rhythm.
Watch from candid port,
alabaster droplets spill
from silver vessels,
overturned at horizons
beyond sightless explanation,
known only
to the Conductor's divine hand,
orchestrating noiseless crescendos
cascading onto scales
of uneven score,
shifting into
soundless,
unique,
glistening notes,
not soon ending for lack of dancing
erratically,
though never disturbing
their fickle partners,
gleefully following the silent,
calming,
clamor
to the finale:

a
  m
    u
     s
    i
      c
       a
       l

keyed in

resounding

        p e a c e.

rly 2011

Summertime

Days are given for smiles and pleasure;
Gay-time vacations
To always remember.
Picnics, a circus, festivals too—
Boat rides, swimming—so much to do!

Pack up suitcases, duffle bags too,
With Gospel tracts—any will do.
Golfing, biking, or pitching a tent—
Tell others for them Jesus was sent.

Lest sunshine 'n rainbows
Blur your vision,
Don't forget God's commission.
Pleasant days are not for our greed—
Souls are lost—His Word they need.

Don't go on vacation
And forget you're a Christian.
Share salvation—
It's a year-round mission!

rly 2008

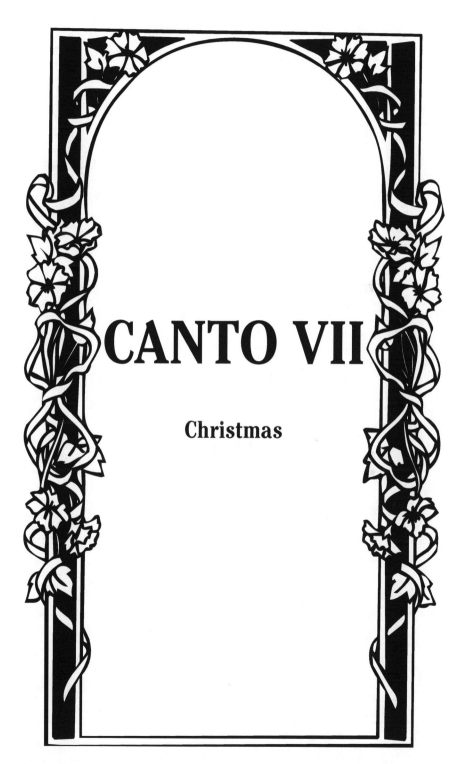

CANTO VII

Christmas

In The Beginning

When did You know
You would be King?
When the star appeared
And angels did sing?

When did You know
The Savior You'd be?
When shepherds came
And magi bowed knee?

When did You know
You were God's Son?
When Simeon cried,
"Lo, He is the One"?

Perhaps You knew,
Seeing Mary's face,
The Promise now sent
For all human race.

God's wondrous plan
No longer concealed.
To all who believe,
His grace now revealed.

Thank You, dear Babe,
O Holy Blest Child.
Deity prayed man
To be reconciled.

rly 2008

The Nativity

Ornaments hung, popcorn strung—
Spices filled the air.
Hearts cared, all shared—
Good will wished everywhere.

Houses all trimmed, candles lit—
Eyes upon the tree.
Hearts filled, joy spilled—
Grace decked Nativity.

Beautiful sight, lovely night—
Beheld God's one Son.
Hearts sang, bells rang—
Love sent—good news had come.

Keep not the Babe 'neath the tree—
Jesus keep in hearts.
Souls live—God gives—
His grace—ever imparts.

rly 2009

Who Would Have Ever Known

Who would have ever known—
An ancient king would leave his throne,
Be a carp'ter's son 'til fully grown
And promise, in death,
A kingdom home?

Who would have ever known—
Could find us 'midst the sin we'd sown,
Whisper kind, "You'll not be alone.
I'll live in your heart
Which once was stone."

. . . and a king became my Savior—
Who would have ever known?

rly 2007

Merry Christmas

Pretty wrappings
'Neath Christmas lights.
Glowing colors make delightful sights.
Unseen gifts—peace, joy, and love
Brought down to man from stars above.
Embrace them all this yuletide season.
Celebrate Jesus—
Christmas' true reason.

rly 2002

The Dawn Of Redemption

Hasten to see the babe in the stable.
Pillowed hay low ox and cow.
Accolades strain—wise men bow.
Seraphim hail to all who are able.

Prophets foretold the Son of Jehovah.
Star is set to guide our way.
Reparation—come this day.
He'll be our King—glory hallelujah!

Blissful hearts will ever remember.
Render thanks for that glad morn.
Favoring all—Jesus born.
God became man one day in December.

rly 2008

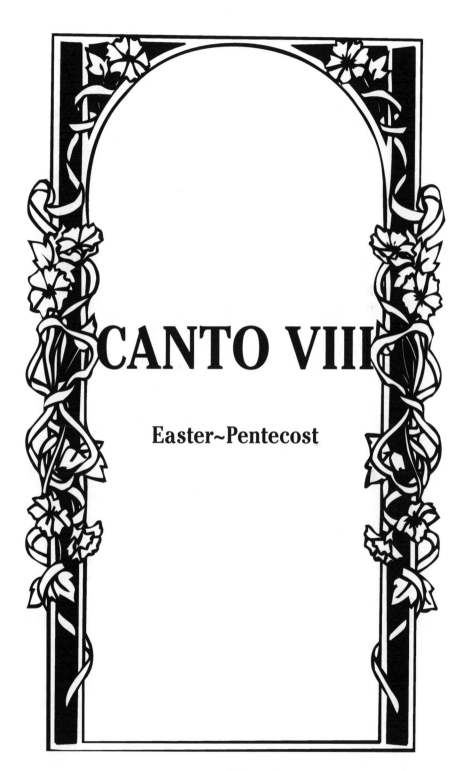

CANTO VIII

Easter~Pentecost

Will You?

Look to His hands—nailed to the tree;
Painfully driven for you and me.

Look to His feet—both bound and worn;
Sanctified wholly to bear the scorn.

Look to His side—blood flows to ground;
Acutely piercing—a woeful sound!

Look to His eyes—compassion, love;
Forbearing mercy from whence above.

Look to His heart—God's will to find;
Incessant favor—your life and mine!

Father has done all that He could
For all to believe—if only we would.
rly 2008

Pomp And Circumstance

Attend the throngs that have come
Hailing laud this unknown son.
Babes in arms—the agéd too—
Waving palms while passing through;
Hopes a king has come at last—
Knowing not lots be cast.

Prefer this crowd cheer or cry
When again He passes by.
Thorns adorn a bloody head;
Bears a cross—to Calv'ry led.
"Where's deliv'rance—where's our King?
Laud our praise we did sing."

Depleting life hung to die.
Abating faith will ask why.
"Father, forgive"—head draped low.
"I'll rise again—then they'll know."
rly 2003

Crown Him, Crown Him

Days of old, hosannas did ring.
A nation thought they had a king.
Scattered fronds decored His feet—
City of David came to greet.

On ashen colt rode through the gate;
"Is He the one long we did wait?"
Jeweled crest He did not wear—
Lone the face of a servant bear.

Now, as then, hosannas still ring.
Esteem aloud we have our King.
Commendations at His feet—
The Savior has come—Him we greet.

No more the Lamb for sin He bleeds.
He died—arose—now intercedes.
Gilded crown—white garment wear—
The image of God He does bear.

rly 2005

And If I Be Lifted Up

Do you see the Lamb—sacrificed?
Bore scourge on the tree—
Relief for you and me.
'Twas God's own—Jesus Christ.

Do you see the Lamb—sacrificed?
Counts torment for gain—
Through love exhibits pain.
'Twas God's own—Jesus Christ.

Do you see the Lamb—sacrificed?
Divine turns aside—
In Him we can abide.
'Twas God's own—Jesus Christ.

Do you see the Lamb—sacrificed?
Unsoiled from the ground—
Wears purple and a crown.
'Tis th' Savior—Jesus Christ.

rly 2004

Pentecost

One hundred twenty knelt
Behind locked doors one day.
In one accord of mind and soul,
They soon began to pray.
A roaring sound of mighty winds
At once did fill the air.
To know from where it came so quick,
They truly knew not where.
Swiftly flames like fire appeared
And rested on each head.
With strange tongues began to speak—
Still knowing what was said.
Amazed were some,
While others mocked,
That these were drunk with wine.
But, oh—one hundred twenty knew—
'Twas God's appointed time.

A man called Peter stood
To lift his voice and speak,
"Ye men of Israel hear these words:
Salvation you must seek.
A man approved by God did come—
By mighty signs He came.
Delivered up by wicked hands—
Then crucified and slain.
But who you buried God raised up—
And they are one the same.
Jehovah made Him Lord and Christ—
Yes, Jesus is His name!
Now whosoever will be found
Can flee from sin's dark hour.
Repent and God will fill you with
The Pentecostal power."
rly 2010

Ablaze

Burn all dross—start a fire in me.
O, Holy Ghost, let flames run free.

Let it begin—let it be new.
Rekindle Spirit; I in You.

Life consume—with You, now fill.
Use me only for Your will.

Constant each day—every hour;
Burn in me Pentecost power.

rly

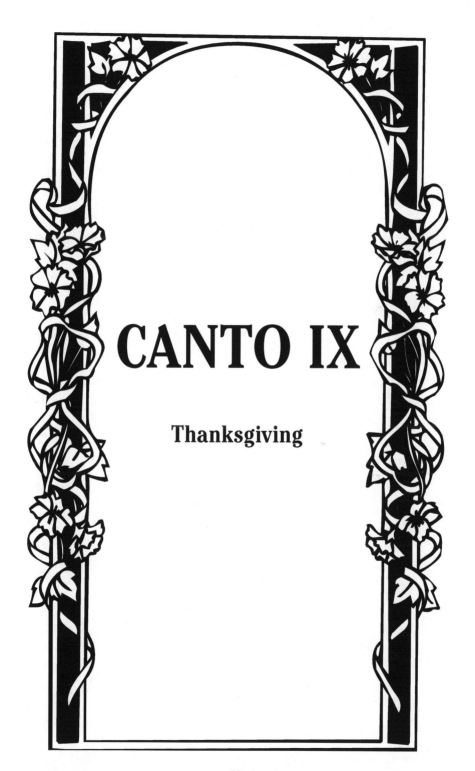

CANTO IX

Thanksgiving

God's Gifts

Let us be thankful
For what God has done.
Gave us Jesus—His only Son.

His true Holy Word
To be read each day.
Gave His Spirit to guide life's way.

Earth's bounty and boon
Ours daily in full.
Gave His power to reign, to rule.

Who is like God to give you and me
Unmerited gifts
So rich, so free.

rly 2003

Thankworthy

Grateful for the way back home—
A bloodstained road—died alone.

Grateful for when thinking twice—
The Savior still—Jesus Christ.

Grateful for the fixed love shown—
Set all accounts—black seeds sown.

Grateful for the empty grave—
Emptied Hades—once it's slave.

Grateful for the way back home—
Never again need we roam.

rly 2001

Now Give I Thanks

For valleys low You take me through,
For mountain tops You lead me to,
For songs of praise I sing to You—
Now give I thanks for all You do.

For peace of mind when ere confused,
For constant love while some refused,
For mercy sure when grace abused—
Now give I thanks for all You do.

For presence known though left alone,
For faith to trust my sin atoned,
For hope to stay Your Promised Home—
Now give I thanks for all You do.

rly 2003

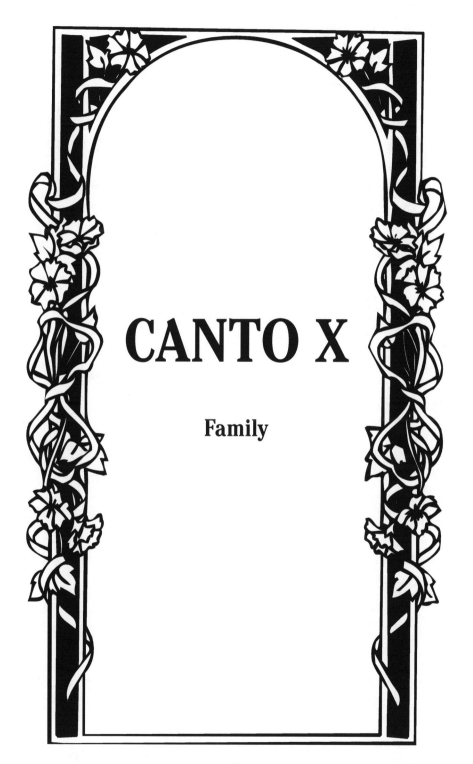

CANTO X

Family

Anticipation
written for granddaughter, Abigail

Little sister's coming home.
I sit waiting all alone.
Will she look just like me?
I can't wait to finally see!

Love her lots—get along fine.
Be her best friend—she'll be mine.
Sing some songs, play all day.
Tell her God takes sin away.

Tell her Jesus came from Heaven.
I'm so smart—though only seven!
I asked God to make all right.
Thank Him when I pray tonight.

Listen!
Little sister's coming home!
I won't have to play alone.
Will she look just like me?
I can't wait to finally see!

rly 2004

Amber's Song
song written for daughter, Amber

I love you and you love me—
That's the way God meant it to be.

He gave us a heart—a heart of love.
Kind of love that's from Heav'n above.

He gave us a song—a song of praise.
Sing for Him 'til the end of our days.

He forgave our sin—He saved our souls.
Gave a reason for living
When He made us whole.

rly 1971

Unbroken Circle

Walking your High way,
All I say and do.
Long family will see,
Desire You too.

Wanting to serve You
Each day more and more.
Praying my children
See grace that is sure.

Paths of decision
Will come into sight;
Want them to choose
What's been given as right.

Have read them Your Word
To keep in their hearts;
Trust in salvation
And never depart.

rly 1989

Commitment

The husband is loved with all the heart.
From Him is vowed to never depart.
Children are loved and rightly adored.
Blessings from Thee—
Could ask for no more.

But Jesus is loved with all the soul.
He cleanses within to make one whole.
To Him is owed all being, all life.
Helps each to be
Good mother and wife.

Constantly pray to Father above:
Do bless all mine with mercy and love.

rly 1989

Birthday Girl
written for granddaughter, Allison

Guess who it is
That just turned one?
A pretty little girl named Allison!

Play lots of games—
Eat ice cream and cake.
Ask Mommy for lots of pictures to take.

Blow out your candle—
Wish for just you.
May all your dreams one day come true.

rly 2006

"Mama"
written for mother, Mary Wilma Westlake

Shallow breath, ebbing strength;
Age hugs your face.
Mem'ries stored years ago—
An endearing place.

A little girl was I,
With a fevered brow.
You sat close beside me—
The same as I do now.

Scrapes 'n bumps didn't hurt
When you'd hold me tight.
Oh, I long to hold you—
Keep you close this night.

Hands of time move quickly;
Never more to past.
God's voice beckons you—
Our lives went by too fast.

Yet we know our Savior's love
Binds eternally.
So when you kneel before Him nigh—
Save a place for me.

rly 2002

The Arrival

Mary Wilma Westlake, 2/27/22-9/5/02

Angels came to take my mama
'Twixt dew of dawn and night.
They carried her to grandeur home
On silvered wings of flight.

Now she breathes celestial air
And beholds her Savior's face.
She knows full well the love of God
And His amazing grace.

rly 2002

Big Boy
written for grandson, Christian Jacob

My name is C. J.—
I'm no longer bound.
I'm learnin' to go
When my feet hit the ground!

Today's my birthday—
I just became one.
I'm a toddler boy
And havin' such fun!

Walkin' 'n runnin'—
I gotta explore.
Hey—did you just shout,
"Don't open that door!"

Things that go gr-r-r—
Mud puddles 'n worms
Keeps Ma on her toes
As she screams 'n squirms!

God is my buddy—
Stays near where I go.
Jesus, keep me safe.
Bless me as I grow!

rly 2009

Mother's Bible

In a fairer land
I sit with my Lord;
To read no more—
Behold the Living Word.

This Bible's been read
Many times through.
Now pass it on
And give it to you.

Never gave up—
Was proven while tried.
Tears that fell
On it's pages—now dried.

Promises marked
Of what God would do.
Claimed them all—
He was faithful and true.

Be steady—hold fast.
I'll see you soon
When you journey past
The stars and moon.

To Glory Land,
Together we'll be,
With One who died
For you and me.

rly 2009

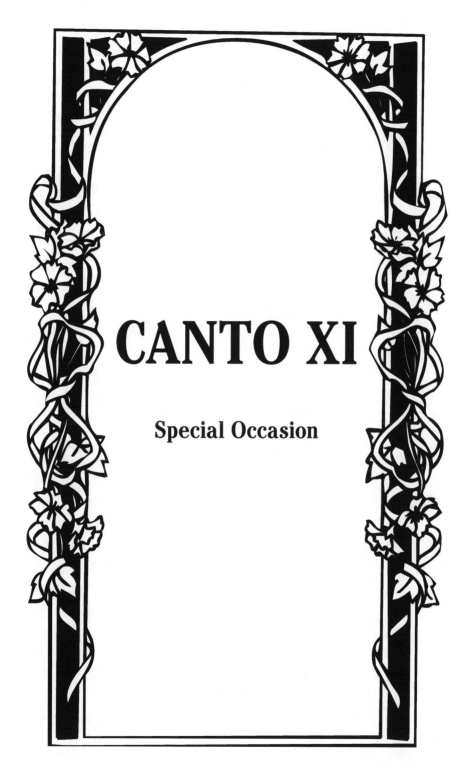

CANTO XI

Special Occasion

Necessities

Seems a long time—soon be on my way.
Sending requests—
My "Baby Shower" Day.

Diapers, wipies, baby soap, lotion—
Something to help
With that "gas" commotion!

Aspirin for fevers—blanket for bed.
Don't forget cream
So my bottom's not red!

Bring any item mentioned above.
Mommy will thank you—
Your gift of love.

rly 2008

Wedding Blessing

A three-strung cord
Not easy does part.
The tie that binds
Is Christ in your heart.

While you journey
Husband and wife,
Let God guide
This new path of life.

God bless your love
Each day, each night.
Seek only *His* will—
Your's will be right.

rly 2008

Thank You

"Thank You" seems so little to say
For kindness shown a special way.

I'm so blest to have friends like you.
Phone calls, cards—a visit or two.

Flowers sent; a homemade meal—
How can I express thanks I feel?

So from the heart
Come words of rhyme:

Lord, bless each one—
These friends of mine.

rly 2001

Mother's Day

Mother's Day is a blessing to me
Since God made you my mother to be.

I pray God's goodness
The whole day through.
For never there was
A mother like you.
rly 2000

Graduation

Dreamin', schemin', an idea or two;
To figure it out—a hard thing to do.
Trustin' yourself is not always right.
God can guide you—He'll be your light.

Plans for you He has promised for good.
Asks you do what only you should.
On journey of life you'll need a friend.
Jesus is here—on Him depend.
rly 2008

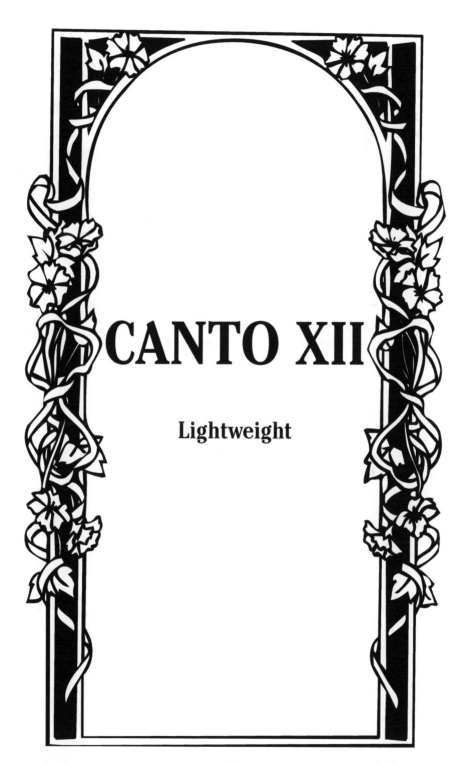

CANTO XII

Lightweight

Welcome

Come in, sit down, have some tea.
Friends are such good company.
Neighbor came the other day—
Just dropped by—couldn't stay.

Dust bunnies, too, welcome you.
Weightless, fluffy—naught to do.
Quiet, friendly—they don't hide—
Loiter close—by your side!

Don't pay them heed—they'll not stay.
Find that broom—*just not today!*
rly 2011

Caution

If with toys you want to play,
Chances are that you might pay.
For when you play you could break—
So please don't touch for goodness sake!
rly 1990

Helen's Place
written for friend, Helen Montgomery

She'll trim your locks, curl your tresses,
Show you hats that match the dresses.
Colored beads to weave in your hair,
Purses, sandals, sneakers for wear.

Best of all there are wigs galore.
Lookin' fine when you leave her store!
Short wigs, long wigs, curly, straight.
Special orders—ne'er to wait.

Remembers mom with neighbor girls.
And, like mom, she'll do your curls.
Maebelle's Wigs®—the place to go—
Full attire from head to toe.
rly 2006

Ode To June
title request by friend, June.

Hey diddle, diddle!
I've a bulge in my middle
And I hope to whittle it soon.
But eating's such fun,
I won't get it done—
'Til my dish runs away with my spoon!
rly

Setting The Pace

A by-gone team of Yellow 'n Green
Has emerged on top
As the "come-back team."
Fans are faithful
To the Pack of Green Bay—
Believe their guys can win the day!

Lombardi knew just what to do
To bring the vic'try—pull them through.
Coaches come; coaches go.
They do their best to top the show.

Seasons roll—they're in, they're out.
Coming back—what it's about.
With team effort, drive down the line.
Gainin' reputation—oh, so fine!

Cheeseheads believe
In their Green 'n Yellow—
Colors donned by each fellow.
So hold to your seats—
They'll be back—
Football team of the Wisconsin "Pack"!

rly 2002

Mr. Music Man

written for Don George

Always "put up" with us—
Never "gave up" on us.

Times of less practice
And more of jest;
While learning our notes,
You were put to the test!

Director of music—you were the best.
That's right, Don—better than rest!

Retire, you must—
The baton passes on.
Thanks for the mem'ries
As you led us in song.

rly 2007

Nut Case

Scurry, scurry, little squirrel—
Long bushy tail in a swirl.

Up the tree, down you go—
Hide those nuts before the snow.

Look around—others can't see—
The treasures you bury are just for thee.

rly 2003

Rain, Rain, Rain

Gotta find a mountain—run as I go.
My t.v.'s floatin' in the den below!

All the fishies 'n frogs under the sea
Are now in my house
Swimmin' round me!

This rain has been
Since I don't know when—
Will ever the sun show its face again?

Any more rain and I'm sure to drown—
Seen any gopher wood bobbin' around?

Behold now a lake
Where once was a park.
Gotta find a hammer—build me an ark!
rly 2011